EVERYBODY GETS STINKY FEET

Advance Praise for
EVERYBODY GETS
STINKY FEET

"Jim Cosgrove has come a long way from the young man mowing my yard to an inspiring writer. This book captures a genuine sense of life's important moments and the joys and trials life can throw your way."

— George Brett, Kansas City Royals legend and
National Baseball Hall of Famer

"It is exciting for me to discover the adult Jim Cosgrove and observe his potential realized as a modern philosopher. This anecdotal collection of experiences and memories will relate to everyone who has been influenced by a parent or has raised a child. This little book is a perfect handbook for marriage prep. The stories are short and humorous, but carry a deep resounding message. "I choose love" could well be Jim's mantra."

— Sister Jeanne O'Rourke, RSM, Jim's sixth grade teacher,
who knows good writing and a well-diagrammed sentence

"Through song and storytelling, Jim Cosgrove has captured the hearts and minds of kids and parents all across the country. Kansas City is lucky to call him one of our own, and I'm so grateful for his work helping kids learn meaningful life lessons in a fun and creative way."

— Mayor Sly James, Mayor of Kansas City, Missouri

"Jim Cosgrove's *Everybody Gets Stinky Feet* is a warmhearted common sense guide to living life to the happiest and ethically fullest. We could all benefit from Jim's tender wisdom, and the even greater wisdom he's received from his wonderful wife and young daughters."

— Mark Olshaker, documentary filmmaker,
novelist and coauthor of *Mindhunter* and *Obsession*

"Jim Cosgrove is one of those alien beings who just naturally makes others happy. I don't know how he does it. You spend five minutes with him and you walk away thinking, 'Why am I so happy now? I wasn't happy before.'

Every essay in *Everybody Gets Stinky Feet* is like spending those five minutes with Jim. You read about him comparing his own parenting to Mike Brady or finding another word to use that doesn't start with "F" or challenging us to find our own super powers and you find yourself feeling happy. It's like Jim can't help but circulate joy.

It's one of the great joys of my life that I have gotten to know Jim a little bit. My daughters grew up singing along with him. I've appreciated and used some of his thoughts about baseball ... and life. Jim's a treasure, and his book is pure, concentrated Jim Cosgrove, no additives or preservatives."

— Joe Posnanski, #1 New York Times best-selling
author of *Paterno* and *The Soul of Baseball.*

"Jim Cosgrove lives and writes from his heart. You will want to follow him, "stinky feet" and all, wherever he goes in this lovely, easy-to-read collection of essays about being human on a daily basis."

— Phyllis Theroux, essayist, columnist,
and author of *The Journal Keeper: A Memoir*

"If you dive into this book expecting a good laugh, you'll be amply rewarded. But don't be surprised if you also come away with a few tears and a greater understanding that we all have experiences that unite us. Like stinky feet."

— Martin W. Schwartz, *Missouri Life* magazine

"Wonderful! Jim's book is filled with positive messages that shine in a world longing for some light. His stories will warm your heart."

— Steve Potter, Director and CEO,
Mid-Continent Public Libraries

EVERYBODY GETS STINKY FEET

Uplifting Essays
About The Sweet
AND SMELLY
Bits Of Life

JIM COSGROVE

Mighty Mo Productions
Prairie Village, KS

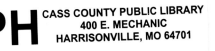

Published in the United States of America by

Mighty Mo Productions
PO Box 8156
Prairie Village, KS 66208
www.mightymoproductions.com

Cover and text design: Rob Peters www.rob-peters.com
Illustrations: Charlie Mylie @popupcharlie
Author photo: David Shaughnessy www.shaughnessyphoto.com

ISBN 978-0-9986076-0-3

Printed in the USA

CONTENTS

BUT FIRST, THESE WORDS FROM THE AUTHOR...

On our first date, Jeni heard a voice in her head that told her I was the guy she would marry.

Seriously. Right there at the table on the patio of the Jerusalem Café while we were still working on a platter of falafel and baba ganoush.

It wasn't your ordinary day-dreamy "Hey, I wonder if this could lead to something long term" kind of voice. It was a formal voice – loud and definitive.

"You have met the man you are going to marry," it said.

But it didn't freak her out as much as you might think, because she'd heard the voice before at pivotal points in her life.

It was the same voice that years earlier had told her, "Go, and hug your sister. This may be the last time you see her." And it was.

It was the same voice that spoke to her about a month before we met, when she was finally getting clarity after an unhealthy relationship and was wondering what was next for her. It said to her, "Don't worry, he's right around the corner." And I was.

I'm grateful she peeked around that corner and it didn't freak her out. And I'm especially grateful that she didn't tell me about the voice that night. If she had, I would have bolted for the parking lot, and it's a good bet we never would have fallen in love, and we never would have married and had kids, and I never would have had material to write a parenting column for the *Kansas City Star*, and you wouldn't be reading this right now.

So, like many things in life, I owe the success of this project to Jeni and her intuition. She trusts it, and so do I.

● ● ● ●

We all have scads of stories to tell. And these are some of my stories. They come from the heart. And while I wrote them primarily for my own enjoyment, it sure is fun to share them with others.

Most of these essays come from my time as a parenting writer for *The Kansas City Star*. My work first appeared on the *Star's* online *Mom-2-Mom* blog, where I was the lone daddy voice. Eventually I was invited to be one of four monthly parenting columnists for the *Star's* online and print editions.

The title of this collection is a line from my song "Stinky Feet," which is also the title of my second album. "Everybody gets stinky feet," has become one of the main tenets of my vocation as a family entertainer.

And, as I remind the kids, the song is not about making fun of stinky feet. It celebrates stinky feet! There's no shame in it.

Each person on the planet in the course of a lifetime experiences stinky feet – literally and/or figuratively. "Stinky feet" can be any one of the many sometimes messy, sometimes odiferous bits that make us human. It's a reminder that life is regularly untidy and confusing. And that's not only OK – it can be the very thing that makes life interesting. Our primal smelliness is one of the many things we share as a species. And I like to focus on stuff we have in common.

Kids seem to get this right away. Many adults, however, have forgotten the reality of their inherent stinkiness, or simply have chosen to deny it – including my mother.

Shortly after I wrote my song "Stinky Feet," I played it for her. "Oh my," she said shaking her head with her face pruned into a disapproving wince. "That's awful. Nobody's going to want to hear that. It'll never sell." She was not known for her diplomacy.

I knew I must be on to something good if my mom didn't like it. When I released the song, the kids loved it. "Stinky Feet" would go on to sell more than 20,000 copies (not bad by indie standards), and the music video has hundreds of thousands of views.

When my band and I performed "Stinky Feet" with the Kansas City Symphony at the world-class Kauffman Center for the Performing Arts, my mother was in the audience. As I introduced the song from the stage, I told the story of her initial underwhelming reaction.

"Mom, I bet you never thought you'd hear this song done by an 80 piece orchestra," I said. "This is for you."

She later admitted with a hint of pride in her voice, "I suppose it's pretty good after all. Of course the symphony helps a lot."

The song took on a life of its own and would eventually come to define my career. That was never the plan. In fact, I didn't have a plan at all. I was just writing songs for my nieces and nephews and recording and performing because it was fun. I knew nothing about the music business or really anything about music. I had just taught myself to play a few cowboy chords on the guitar and started composing simple ditties. I never set out to make it a career. It just unfolded before me, and I took one faith-filled step at a time. And here I am.

Early in my career, a good friend of mine who was a second grade teacher told me, "If you want to get kids laughing, just mention underwear or stinky feet." And I'm not so sure it was a conscious decision, but, looking back, that's the premise from where I started writing.

One of the greatest gifts I received from my young fans is my name "Mr. Stinky Feet." I didn't come up with the name myself. I'm not that clever. And it wasn't the product of focus group testing. It just came about organically. After my second album came out, kids started calling me "Stinky Feet."

I still remember the day it really sunk in. I was high-fiving a bunch of students in the hallway of a school where I'd just performed an assembly. A few kids started calling out, "Hey, Stinky Feet! Yo, Stinky Feet!" And I playfully shouted back, "Hey, that's "Mister Stinky Feet" to you!" It somehow sounded more respectable.

The name stuck, so I decided to embrace it. Kids identify with it. It's easy to remember. And it suits me.

Once I was contacted by a theater manager who was wavering about putting my stage name on the marquee because he thought it might be too low-brow. "Don't you think it might turn some people off?"

"Maybe," I said, "but tell me this, are people more likely to take a second look at a marquee that reads 'Jim Cosgrove' or 'Mr. Stinky Feet?'"

Since showbiz tends to favor the curious, he opted for the feet.

In the end, the name may indeed be a bit uncultured and lean a little toward crass, but it has opened doors for me. But what's really cool is it reminds me to be more childlike (not childish) in everything I do.

With a name like Mr. Stinky Feet, I just can't take myself too seriously.

PART I
ALL-STARS AND OTHER COOL PEOPLE

MEMORIES ROOTED IN GEORGE BRETT'S LAWN

My love affair with baseball and the Kansas City Royals predates the glory of 1985 and the near-glory of 1980. It goes back to a time before free agency and the strikes and obscene salaries. Even before Morganna, the Kissing Bandit.

It started with my father, who would listen to nearly every game on the radio. He would scribble notes next to the box scores in the morning paper. And a few times a year he'd pack up my siblings and me and take us all out to "the ballpark," as he called it.

Then one evening in the spring of 1978 my father came home from work with news that elevated my baseball fever to a new pitch.

All-star third baseman George Brett was moving into our neighborhood – within walking distance of our house. This was beyond huge. In the eyes of a sports-crazed seventh grader, George Brett was about as big and cool as the

Six Million Dollar Man and Evel Knievel rolled into one.

It turned out my dad had a friend who worked for the Royals and was responsible for finding someone to cut Brett's lawn. My dad said if I wanted it, the job was mine. No interview. No mowing test. I was in.

When the day came to meet George and talk business, my dad coached me to play it cool and remain professional.

"Remember you're there to cut his grass," he said. "Don't take advantage of your position by asking for an autograph or bringing your friends around." Staying cool would be extremely difficult considering I would be face to face with a guy who had made a cameo appearance on Fantasy Island.

When I arrived, I was greeted by his signature gap-toothed grin and a Major League hand shake that engulfed my Little League hand. I surveyed his yard and figured it would take less than an hour to cut both the front and back.

"Is 20 bucks all right?" I asked, thinking I might be pushing my luck. No problem.

As I finished up that first day, he handed me $40. There must have been some mistake. "$20 for the front and $20 for the back, right?" he said with a wink.

Thus began one of the most memorable years of my life. I not only cut and bagged grass clippings for an All-Star, I landed one of the sweetest middle-school-kid perks ever – I got to clean up after a few of the epic parties at his bachelor pad that he shared with two other Royals' players. The reality of picking up empty bottles, cups, and cans and wiping up spills wasn't all that thrilling, but this was the stuff that made for legendary school cafeteria stories.

George paid me well and regularly gave me tickets to games. But when he offered me one of his extra ball gloves — a deluxe, major league model, I humbly declined, remembering my father's advice about playing it cool. I'm still kicking myself for that.

But when he cleaned out his locker at the end of the '78 season, after another heartbreaking playoff loss to the Yankees, George gave me one of

his bats. The number 5 was scribbled on the handle, a smudge of pine tar on the grip. He would autograph it for me years later, and I still have it.

George moved out of our neighborhood before the following spring, on to a bigger and better home that fit his rising superstar salary. Although my time with him was brief, I remained a faithful follower.

As I grew older, I continued to scan the daily box scores with the same fanaticism of a child, hoping that he'd gone four-for-four the night before, hoping he'd pull out another .390 season, another batting title, and another pennant. And when they squeaked out a World Series title in 1985, I was thrilled for George most of all. It would have been an injustice to have had such a phenomenal career and not wear a championship ring.

So, George, thanks for the memories of my fist pouch of chewing tobacco, for that $40 tip you once gave me, and for those tickets to see you play the Rangers in Arlington.

But thanks most of all for the 20 full seasons of inspiring, exhilarating, breathtaking, homers-to-the-right-field-bullpen baseball. You have forever bonded me to a game that I always will watch with the enthusiasm and devotion of a 12-year-old. Cooperstown deserves you.

(A version of this essay first appeared in *The Albuquerque Journal* following George Brett's retirement from baseball in September 1993, and this revised version appeared in *The Kansas City Star* following his induction into the National Baseball Hall of Fame in January 1999.)

LIFE HAPPENS ON THE BUS

Last Saturday night I rode the bus home from Irish Fest and took a seat next to a guy slumped against the window. He lifted his head when I sat down, and with a weary voice he said, "Hello."

We exchanged pleasantries, and, although he appeared groggy, if not a bit defeated, he seemed somehow resigned to talk.

He was heading in to work the overnight shift as an assistant manager at a grocery store -- his eighth day in a row. He hoped to get a day off later in the week.

His manager was a jerk and a tyrant, just like so many managers he'd known. And now, that he was working his way up in management, he vowed never to treat his team that way. Only with respect, he said. Then he was silent.

After sitting in the lull of a few quiet minutes, he suddenly spoke, softly and sadly, "My sister passed today."

It took me a second to register the weight of his words. A dozen possible responses flitted through my head, but they all sounded trite or insufficient for something so fresh, so raw, so vulnerable.

Rather than offering my sorrow or some rote condolence, my voice and my brain conspired to form a sentence that seemed to come from somewhere else.

"Tell me about her."

With those words, his hunched shoulders relaxed and his tone turned wistful. He and his sister were close. She was 57. Much older than him, but still close. She suffered a stroke and had been in a coma for a while. Surely his boss would give him time off for the funeral so he could be with his family and celebrate her life.

"Because that's what it's about, right?" he said. "Family. Remembering. Celebrating."

The bus brakes squealed, and he stood up. "This is my stop," he said, shaking my hand. "Thank you." Then he stepped off the bus into the late summer darkness.

This was one of those brief and intense encounters that are so poignant that it can leave you wondering if it really just happened.

I believe that gentle, grieving man was an angel sent to give me a gift – a nudge to help me squirm loose of my comfortable, insulated life and keep my heart and mind wide open.

He reminded me that there are all sorts of people on this giant bus we call earth. They may not all dress like us or talk like us or think like us, but each one has a story to tell. Each one has hopes, fears, joy, and pain. And each is worthy of our respect, because we're all on this journey together. Even though some get off at the next stop, some transfer, and some ride to the end of the line, we're all still brothers – still sisters – still family.

HEAVENLY CHALLAH

Every week Ray bakes bread in the kitchen of Congregation Beth Shalom in Overland Park, Kansas.

He bakes lots of bread. Forty-eight loaves this week – 64 last week. And it's not just any bread, it's "heavenly challah" sent to him as a gift by his lovely departed wife Frieda – in a literal and spiritual sort of way.

"For 50 years I was married to the most wonderful woman in the world," says the 85-year-old Ray with a glint in his eye. "Every Friday she would make fresh challah for our evening meal, and every week the kids would tell her, 'Mom, this is the best challah you've ever made.' This went on for 30 or 40 years."

Twelve years ago Frieda passed away and left Ray broken-hearted. He shuffled around for the next several months grieving and feeling sorry for himself, until the day he decided to do something about it. He looked around and spotted her recipe box in the kitchen.

"I wondered if there was something in there I could make that would help me feel close to her," says Ray. "I came across her challah recipe and thought, 'This is it!'"

He knew how to cook, but had never baked anything, not even a box cake. He went to the store, gathered all the ingredients, and gave it a go. The bread turned out perfectly.

"So, I started to bake. And I felt like she was right there helping me."

Ray was active in a synagogue in St. Louis that ordered expensive challah from a local bakery each week. To help them save money, he volunteered to start baking for the congregation. The bread was a hit and people started asking him to bake challah for their families. A woman in the congregation offered to buy a commercial mixer, and Ray increased his output.

Fortunately for the folks at Congregation Beth Shalom, Ray moved to Overland Park earlier this year. And now he dons his apron and oven mitts every week and embarks on his volunteer labor of love. The challah is used in services every week and is sold as a fund raiser for the congregation preschool.

"If it weren't for this bread, I'd be a tottering old man," he laughs as he leans over and pulls another four loaves out of the oven.

After it cools, the bread is sealed in bags and labeled with a sticker that proudly reads, "Frieda's Heavenly Challah".

And it tastes like heaven. I got a warm sample right out of the oven, and I brought a loaf home for lunch. Between Jeni and me, we ate more than half of it.

If you're in the neighborhood, drop by and buy some for yourself. Ray will thank you and Frieda will bless you.

(In gratitude for the life of Ray Davidson 1923-2015)

ONE BRAVE ANGEL

Just when you think the world can't get any crazier, somehow it does.

And just when you feel you can't bear it any more, you meet someone who can bring the crazy train to a screeching halt. Someone who can make time stand still, if only for a second.

Maybe this person commands your attention with just the right words or a perfectly timed smile or an otherwise inconsequential brush against your forearm. Whatever it is, this person fills you with a burst of hope that everything is not as bad as it seems. This person induces clarity that momentarily restores your faith in humanity. Suddenly you realize that crawling back into bed and burying your head in the pillows isn't such a great option after all.

I call these people angels and messengers and sages. And they're everywhere. Once you get in the habit of recognizing them, you see them more and more frequently. Three weeks ago, I met such an angel.

I was performing for a group of patients and their families at Children's Mercy Hospital. As the kids came into the room — some in parents' arms, some in wheelchairs, some connected to IV poles — I asked them a question I ask most kids when I meet them: "What's your superpower?"

"Flying!" said a boy who was propped up on pillows in a blue wagon.

"Ice," shouted a little girl in a hospital gown. And when I tilted my head and asked how that worked, she said, "I shoot ice out of my fingers." Oh, right, the "Frozen" generation.

And then I came to a girl who was about 8 years old. She was sitting in the front row. When I asked about her superpower, she paused and looked at the floor. And then as she lifted her head, she quietly and confidently declared, "Being brave."

"Wow," I said. "That's an impressive power."

She locked eyes with me and slowly nodded, saying, "Ever since I came here, I've had to be brave."

And then she ever so slightly glanced and tilted her head toward a boy sitting next to her who was recovering from extensive reconstructive surgeries on each of his limbs, and she said with the insight and compassion of a sage, "There are a lot of kids here who have the same superpower as me."

There are no words when you're in the presence of awe-inspiring wisdom. I silently nodded in respect and admiration.

It seems that when I most need a spiritual jolt, it comes from a child. Children are closer to the source than adults. They're intuitive and inherently compassionate. They do not feign affection or interest. They haven't been jaded by cynics or clouded by dogma. They know no labels. They know only love.

I need more angels like her in my life. I need her innocence when faced with the realities of hatred. I need her compassion to help me face my own prejudices. I need her resonating love to offset the fear mongers who spin their deception and hysteria.

In our brief interaction, she reminded me that love brings light to darkness, surrounds hatred, and forces it to surrender. Love reigns supreme.

As I finished up my last song, I turned to thank her, but she was gone. It wasn't a large room with many people. Surely I would have seen her leave, but she must have slipped out during my performance without me noticing.

Angels are known for that.

PRISON CELLS AND GRATITUDE

I didn't spend last Valentine's Day with my wife. But, with her encouragement, I arranged for another date that night.

At about the time we might have been sitting down to a candle-lit dinner, I stood nervously at the entrance to the federal Leavenworth Detention Center as the razor-wired gates rattled shut behind me. I was there to see a prisoner I didn't even know. Not exactly my idea of romantic.

Two weeks earlier I had received a call from an old friend I hadn't spoken to in 15 years. She asked if I would visit her cousin's son, Hank, who had been transferred from a prison in California to this corporately run holding facility while he awaited trial.

He had no friends or family nearby and was frightened and lonely. She thought a visitor from the outside might lift his spirits. I was honored that she thought of me.

The details of Hank's arrest and incarceration are a minor part of the story. What's important is that he is a beautiful, gentle, and resilient soul who was being held in a prison 1,800 miles away from his wife and 9-year-old daughter.

Over the next several months, I visited Hank every few weeks. It was just like I had seen in the movies. He sat on one side of the thick bulletproof glass in his orange scrubs talking over a crackling phone line about how much he missed his family. His most heart-wrenching struggle was how to be an effective and involved father from behind bars.

He detailed his daily claustrophobic routine in a 10-by-20-foot cell with six other guys and one toilet — a far cry from his idyllic life in the mountains of Northern California where he and his wife operated an inn.

I sat on my side of the glass listening and appreciating my pedestrian, suburban existence and trying not to look too "free."

As he struggled to adjust to his new normal, Hank's tears and fears slowly turned into acceptance and, eventually, serenity. He started meditating and exercising regularly. He began to appreciate the little blessings in each day, like sunlight on his face during his brief fresh air time in the yard. He practiced yoga, for which his block mates ridiculed him, until they noticed how calmly he was able to thwart the aggression that swirled around them. They eventually asked him to teach them some poses.

As a guy who had been sober for many years, Hank was surprised that there was no AA meeting in the prison, so he asked permission to start one. It became so popular that they had to divide the group into two, and he led both — one in English and one through a Spanish interpreter. Within six months, Hank had become a modern-day Cool Hand Luke — the one the other guys looked up to.

Last month an unexpected miracle happened. Hank was released after serving nearly a year without having had a trial or a sentence. His wife contacted me and asked if I would be there to pick him up and transport him to a hotel near the airport.

I was just as nervous the day of his release as I was the day I met him. I arrived early and paced for a few minutes in the parking lot before heading

in. What an honor and an amazing gift his family had given me. They trusted me to be the one to share in his first moments of freedom.

Inside the florescent-lit waiting room, I finally got to shake his hand and give him a big hug. Two prison officials escorted us into the no-man's land between the two high, razored fences. When we walked out side-by-side through the gates, Hank suddenly stopped, closed his eyes and drew in a long dramatic breath of cool, crisp freedom. I half expected him to fall to his knees and kiss the ground. He didn't, but he opened his eyes, smiled, and with a nod back toward the prison he said, "Those walls and fences — they're all a facade. They never took my freedom."

Hank agreed that Café Gratitude would be a fitting place to celebrate. He beamed like a little kid as we walked into the restaurant. With wide eyes, he seemed to absorb every detail as if he'd just landed on this planet. "It smells fabulous in here, and everyone is so beautiful!"

Indeed, everything was fabulous that night and every person a work of beauty. To experience his wonder and appreciation made me realize that what began as an attempt to lift his spirits ended with him lifting mine far beyond anything I could have imagined.

I love when life yanks me off the comfortable, well-worn path and into new territory, especially when it challenges my prejudices and leaves me a better person.

A MEMORABLE NIGHT IN BRUSSELS

Like so many tragedies, the attacks in Brussels last week became a teachable moment about fear and trust, and how we can't condemn an entire race or religion based on the extreme acts of a few.

This time I had a personal tale to share with my kids about one of the most memorable nights of my life.

About three weeks after the terrorist attacks of Sept. 11, 2001, I embarked on a tour to perform at schools on U.S. military bases in Europe. It was a tense and frightening time for the whole world and an especially uncertain climate for military families getting ready for deployment.

After midnight one Sunday, I stepped off a train in Brussels to find a nearly deserted station. I had to make it to an airport about 40 miles from there to catch a flight to Italy early the next morning, but there were no buses or trains running at that hour.

I was approached by a lone cab driver named Muhammad who said he could take me there, but since it was so far and would take nearly an hour, he would charge me $100. I had no other option.

After he took me by an ATM to get some cash, I settled into the front seat next to him and we set off into the damp night.

There we were, two strangers, a Middle Eastern Muslim and an American Christian, with the raw emotion of the most horrific terrorist attack in either of our lifetimes shrouded around us. We exchanged pleasantries for a few minutes to get a feel for where each of us stood.

Then Muhammad skillfully and sincerely addressed the proverbial elephant by saying, "I am deeply saddened and outraged by the attacks on your people. I too am saddened and outraged that it was Muslims who did this. I hope you know that this is not what we believe."

I thanked him and assured him that I harbored no anger toward him or Muslims in general. I could hear the relief in his voice as he relaxed and told me about his wife and three children and how he came to Europe from Jordan to find a better life for his family.

We talked about politics and religion and peace and how crazy people get in this world and how we all just need to trust and respect each other.

By the time we arrived, it was nearly 2 in the morning and the airport was closed. I paid Muhammad and thanked him for the ride. He asked if I'd be all right waiting outside. I told him I'd slept in worse conditions, and I gathered my guitar and backpack and stretched out on a bench out front. I covered myself as best as I could with my rain jacket to ward off the chilly mist. Even though I was exhausted, I couldn't get comfortable.

After about 10 minutes on the bench, I saw headlights coming around the circle drive. The car stopped in front of my bench and the window rolled down. It was Muhammad.

"I decided that I couldn't just leave you out here in the cold," he said. "Come on, get in. Let me take you somewhere warm and buy you a beer."

So we drove to a nearby American sports bar that was open until 3.

"I thought Muslims didn't drink," I said after we ordered.

He shrugged, "I thought Christians didn't drink."

I shrugged and smiled, "Cheers!"

Although I can't remember everything we talked about, I just know that it felt like I was hanging out with an old friend. That night renewed my hope for humanity.

I have thought about Muhammad hundreds of times since that night. And I kick myself for not getting his address. I wonder how he and his family are doing and if he's still driving a cab and rescuing people in the middle of the night. I wonder if he ever thinks of me.

Someday I would love to track him down and get our families together. I want him to know that his generosity and compassion left a lasting impression on me.

DANCE OF HEALING– DANCE OF PEACE

In the autumn of 1992, as the earth prepared for winter, I prepared for the death of my father. He had been diagnosed with lung cancer in July of that year. Considering he was an otherwise fit, active, 75-year-old non-smoker, this news came as a surprise to all of us.

My dad was a no-nonsense World War II vet who accepted and followed his doctor's orders like an obedient soldier. He slogged through a series of painful surgeries and treatments in August and September with little complaint, but by the last time I saw him in October, the cancer had spread to his brain and would continue its blitz through his body.

I, on the other hand, was not so accepting of the trajectory of my father's disease until a conversation with three strangers helped me settle into a place of peace.

I was living in Albuquerque and frequently visited the Navajo Nation out on the western edge of New Mexico, where I had lived and worked a few years earlier. One October night I was invited to attend a Yeibeichai (yay-ba-chay) Dance or Night Chant, which is a healing ceremony that helps restore balance and harmony among humans and other elements of the universe – animals, plants, weather, earth formations, and celestial objects. Traditional Navajos live in the understanding that if one of these elements is hurting, sick, or out of balance, then we're all affected by that same imbalance. This particular ceremony was for a woman suffering from a malignant skin cancer, and scores of people had driven in from all over the reservation to help restore her health.

It was a moonless, cloudless night. The Milky Way spilled across the heavens, and to the north, close to the horizon, the silhouette of a high mesa was cut out of the splash of stars. As I drove along the red-rutted roads out among the scrub pines, I saw rows of pickup trucks in the distance and a dome of smoke surrounding the woman's home. Two rows of bonfires lined the dancing area that stretched away from her front door for about 20 yards. Dozens of people huddled around each of the sweet-smelling piñon fires to thaw the chill of the high-desert night.

Seven dancers in leather loin skirts stood in a line led by the Yeibeichai – the Talking God. They wore alien-looking gray masks decked with jewelry, feathers, and bells and rounded, protruding mouths made from gourds.

A tribal medicine man blessed the dancers with a dusting of corn pollen, and then sat down in one of the two, deep easy chairs that had been set up in front of the house. The ailing woman, wrapped in a wool blanket of reds, whites, and blacks, sat beside him.

To the thunder of drums and high-pitched incantations, the dancers bobbed-and-stepped and bobbed-and-stepped past the seated woman in a smoky haze of golden bonfire light. Rattles shaking. Muffled chants screaming. Hypnotic rhythms resonating in my gut.

A young boy in a mask followed at the end of the line – spinning and hopping and waving. Then a jester-looking character – a sacred clown – with his face and body painted with black and white stripes appeared from the crowd.

He weaved and pranced around the dancers taunting them with an animal skin and joking with people in the crowd who laughed along with him.

After about a half hour, I had to take a break from the commotion of the crowd and the drumming and the guys selling beer from the beds of their pickups. I walked out into a clearing where I tilted my head back to take in the amazing display of stars. I slowly breathed in the crisp air and slipped deep into thoughts about my father. I don't know how long I had been lost out there among the stars before I was startled by three young Navajo men in their late teens who were suddenly standing right there in the clearing with me.

"Where'd you guys come from?" I asked, clearly flustered.

"From over at the high school. There was a dance tonight," said the tallest one. "Do you have any cigarettes?"

"I don't smoke," I said. But then I remembered a stale cigar that someone had recently given me, and I had tucked into a coat pocket. They eagerly accepted it, and as they passed it among themselves, they asked what I was doing there and if I understood the ceremony.

I admitted my ignorance, so they explained that the healing ceremony was not only for the sick woman, but for all ailing people and for any imbalance in the world. They said they also prayed for healing of the earth.

I told them about my dad and asked if their prayers would be able to help him. They assured me that he already had been included in the ceremonial prayers.

"But don't laugh about the dance or make fun of it," warned the shortest of the three, who was wearing a small towel on his head, like a shepherd in a children's Christmas play. "If anybody laughs about this, they will get sick, and we will be having a dance for them this time next year."

He said Navajos believe that we are all here on this earth for a reason, that we are all warriors on our own paths and that, of course, we must transition when it's time.

"Your dad must die sometime. But when he dies, whenever it is, don't cry," he said. "If you don't cry, then you will assume his power and strength. You will take on his spirit and he will walk with you always. And if there are people who have hated him or talked bad about him, his power will come back to work against them."

"You mean I shouldn't cry at all?" I asked with some disappointment, since I had already cried and knew I would again. He said that I shouldn't let my grief consume me. I must find peace in the fact that his spirit will live on.

The temperature was dropping, so I decided to go back to the warmth of the bonfires. We shook hands, and as we parted, the one with the towel looked at me sincerely and said, "We will pray for your dad. And don't be surprised if he is healed."

On the drive home, a brilliant shooting star ripped through the sky in front of me. The glow of its tail lingered in the sky for more than a second. I didn't know if it was a sign or not, but I had the feeling that all was well.

One month later my father's spirit left his earthly body. Although I cried, I did my best to remember that his spirit was, and always will be, a part of me. And for the record, I'm confident that those three young men were angels.

(This reflection first appeared in the August/September 1994 issue of *Radical Grace*, a newsletter for the Center for Action and Contemplation.)

PART II
DON'T, 'SHOULD' ON YOURSELF (AND OTHER LESSONS)

MIKE BRADY OR BUFFOON?

Several years ago, our daughters became hooked on The Brady Bunch.

They were fascinated by the characters and their 70s outfits and the fact that the family had a rotary dial telephone hanging in their kitchen. They especially loved the theme song, which they sang often and loudly.

My wife and I knew their new passion was serious when our girls started to include the Brady kids in their bedtime prayers and our older daughter dressed like Cindy for Halloween. They both still think that Carol and Mike are the grooviest parents ever.

And who could argue with that, what with Carol wearing her mod skirts and high heels around the house, and Mike in his paisley shirts and plaid sport coats. But beyond their flare for fashion, they were quick-witted, even-tempered, and always prepared to deliver a wise monologue embedded with a monumental life lesson.

They were nothing like real parents.

As a father, I knew I wouldn't stand a chance trying to live up to the standards of a smart, successful, well-rounded guy like Mike Brady. But seriously, TV dads have rarely realistically portrayed the nuances and complexities of fatherhood.

On one end there were super dads like Mike Brady, Ward Cleaver, and Sheriff Andy Taylor, who helped set an unrealistic bar for how a good father should conduct himself.

Then along came the likes of Al Bundy and Homer Simpson, who sent the pendulum swinging in the other direction. Pretty soon sitcoms featured fathers who were portrayed as hapless buffoons, kept out of trouble only by the well-timed actions of their intellectually superior, infinitely patient, and forgiving spouses.

I applaud the fact that TV moms have shaken their June Cleaver images to become stronger and more complex characters. But it seems that in the process, fathers have been relinquished to the role of court jester.

Although I can do some pretty dumb things, I'm pretty sure that I don't have to act foolish in order for my wife to look good. She can shine on her own without my help.

I suppose that ordinary, everyday dads don't make for very good sitcom material.

These are dads who sometimes get overwhelmed and yell and go through periods of serious doubt about whether or not they're being a good father. These are also the dads who consider parenthood an honor and who might actually enjoy changing diapers. These are dads who get their kids dressed in the morning and tie their shoes and dads who let their giggling daughters paint their toe nails. These are stay-at-home dads and dads who work two jobs to pay the bills. These are dads who only see their kids on weekends and dads who are separated from their kids for months or years at a time and still give everything they've got.

Dads don't need TV sitcoms and other media to set the standards of a good father. We already know that some days we're Mike Brady and some days we're Homer Simpson, and most days we're effectively maintaining somewhere in between.

WHO SAYS I CAN'T?

If anyone ever tells you that you can't follow your dreams, don't believe them – not even for a second.

For much of my adult life people have told me, "You can't do that!" or "That'll never work."

My own mother thought I was crazy for writing songs when I barely knew how to play a guitar. And when I first sang "Stinky Feet" for her, she said with her sweet maternal bluntness, "That's awful. It'll never sell."

Since then we've sold tens of thousands of copies of the song, and when she saw me perform it with the Kansas City Symphony, she shrugged and admitted that maybe it wasn't so bad after all.

When my brother Dan and I first went into business together, many raised their eyebrows and shook their heads. One friend said, "Bad idea. My dad and his brothers started a family business and now they don't speak."

Nearly 13 years later, we're still in business – although some months we limp along. And my brother and I still talk.

Shortly after Jeni and I married, she decided to quit her job and work with me. People told her, "You can't work with your husband. You'll drive each other crazy, and your marriage won't last."

What they didn't count on is Jeni and I actually enjoy spending time with each other. It's not always a picnic, but it works, and at the end of the day we still like each other.

When we found out Jeni was pregnant, our friends and family said, "I guess that puts an end to touring together. You can't travel when the baby comes!"

Oh, yeah? Watch us! At eight months pregnant, Jeni was with me at the Dubuque County Fair in Iowa. We traveled with baby Lyda, and she learned how to adapt and ride in a car seat for long distances without a video player.

"OK, fine," they said. "You've done it with one, but you'll never manage traveling with two kids."

Done it. And still doing it. About 17,000 miles on the road together this year. It's crazy and exhausting sometimes. And, yes, there are tears and tantrums and frazzled nerves. But there is also laughter and joy and new people and new experiences and roadside attractions to behold. The important thing is that we're together.

We still run into friends, family, and complete strangers who insist on dispensing advice laced with "can't" and "don't" and "should" and "shouldn't." Some people just expect everyone to be as frightened and anxious as they are.

One of my father's favorite sayings was, "Don't 'should' on yourself." By heeding his advice, my wife and I have learned to smile and nod our heads at the naysayers and plow forward. We know it's just their fear talking – fear of the unknown, fear of failure and, even, fear of success.

And I'm not advocating being a Pollyanna and expecting everything to always work out. I'm talking about following your passions, no matter the outcome.

Success is never guaranteed. But stagnation is certain if you don't ever take a leap of faith.

HOLY CORN BREAD, SISTER!

I made some corn bread for Christmas Eve dinner last year and nobody ate it. Only two pieces were cut from the dish, and they were left uneaten on plates, only to be tossed into the garbage.

The bread was whipped up from one of those mixes that come in a bag. "From Wisconsin," it said on the package. "Organic. Whole grain." And it tasted about as dry and organic as a ground up Wisconsin barn door.

I couldn't bring myself to throw it out, so I wrapped up the remainder to feed to the birds.

Then I remembered a clever baking trick I learned from a bunch of Mother Teresa's nuns I worked with long ago at a soup kitchen in Gallup, New Mexico. It was a lesson in recycling, renewal and revival — a lesson in breathing life back into things destined for the dump. These nuns would

drive all over town to supermarkets and restaurants to pick up any edible discards they could salvage to feed the hungry.

On this day they had a huge box of over- ripe, bruised bananas and loads of bready things — semi-stale sweet rolls, cinnamon buns, dinner rolls, and croissants.

On the floor of the kitchen they placed the biggest mixing bowl I had ever seen — big enough for me to sit in (although I didn't). They had us peel all of the mushy bananas and drop them into the bowl. Then they dumped in all of the dried-up sweet breads and rolls and poured in a couple gallons of milk. Nothing was measured or weighed. They were winging it. And my guess is that these women had spent years winging a lot of things, which is part of what made them so awesome.

One of the nuns handed me a potato masher, and four of us churned up the concoction in the bowl until it was a velvety batter. Then they poured it into about 20 greased bread pans and slid them into their cavernous ovens. The result was delicious, moist banana bread they served to their guests that evening. It was a modern-day loaves and fishes story — turning scraps into a feast.

So, taking a page from the sisters' wing-and-a-prayer cookbook, I crumbled up the dry corn bread into a mixing bowl. I added some milk, a few spoonfuls of applesauce and several shakes of cinnamon and poured it into a couple of baking dishes. It was not only moist, but also really tasty. I was instantly inspired by how this little baking lesson can apply to my life and to my family.

I don't necessarily need to throw out things, situations or relationships in my life just because they get a little dried and crumbly. Maybe I just need to add a little of this and some of that — like a pinch of patience or a dash of a different perspective — and remix it. Maybe I can put some of it on the back burner to simmer. Or maybe I could mash it all up with something sweet and bake it for a while, and then see what comes out.

Sometimes it's best to ignore the recipe and just wing it.

FOR #$%& SAKE, CHOOSE ANOTHER WORD!

Consider the f-word. Yup, that f-word. The granddaddy of all curse words. The exhaustingly exploited f-bomb.

Yes, I've used it. You've probably used it, too. And if you haven't, you've thought about using it.

That emotionally charged word has become a topic of interesting conversation in our house now that school has started.

"I hear that word all the time from the boys in my class," our younger daughter said.

"Yeah, me too," said our sixth-grader. "Third grade was about the time I started to hear it."

While they might hear it more often on the playground and in the cafeteria, it's not like they haven't heard it before at sporting events or from strangers walking down the street.

I'm not particularly offended by the f-word; it's just annoying, like a linguistic gnat. Its overuse renders it meaningless. Like when it's used to describe something awesome and something heinous. How can it be both?

It starts creeping into the lexicon of kids who want to feel cool and empowered, like they're getting away with something. And it pretty much continues to be used by those same kids when they're adults and for the same reasons.

A few years ago, I attended a presentation at work by a well-respected and talented video producer. About 15 minutes into his talk, he dropped an f-bomb, then he paused, and with a mischievous grin said, "It's cool if I use that here, right?" He had the self-satisfied look of a 10-year-old who just got away with passing gas at Thanksgiving dinner.

Despite some squirming and uncomfortable laughter from most of the nearly 100 people in the audience, not one of us was willing to admit to being "uncool." Apparently he took this as an expletive-approving green light.

I started counting how many times he used the f-word and finally gave up after a dozen or so. I soon lost interest in the presentation – because his videos, although impressive, were completely upstaged by his lack of class and his disrespect for a professional environment. Maybe some people found his cavalier attitude refreshing and endearing. I guess I'm just not that cool.

From a grammatical standpoint, I must admit that the f-word has impressive versatility. Although it emerged primarily as a verb, its variations can be used as a noun, adjective, adverb, interjection and an effective intensifier. There aren't many words with that kind of range.

But aside from that, it's a lame and lazy choice. And I find it boring when comedians use it excessively. The most creative and funny people don't have to lean on obscenities and shock to get a laugh.

I can appreciate that the f-word has its place when, say, a hammer falls on your toe. "And I find it almost endearing when I talk with my Irish friends who were weaned on the word and can't help using it in every other sentence. And it's pretty funny when Grandma drops a cuss word at a family gathering and grabs everyone's attention.

As a parent and a lover of language and civility, my appeal to habitual f-bombers is to simply show some respect. We've taught our girls that a person's choice of words is often an indication of how they'll treat others. If people use disrespectful language, they'll likely be disrespectful in other ways.

Words have power. They carry energy, vibrations, and resonance. The f-word has especially low vibration. That's why it's a popular choice in negative energy situations of anger and aggression.

Most people avoid lobbing these word grenades around children and their own mothers. So, why would we not extend the same respect to friends, co-workers, and strangers — or to an audience we were being paid to address?

If you want to grab attention with your language, then consider a creative challenge to try something new. Check out a thesaurus. You'll find thousands of interesting alternatives in there.

WHAT'S YOUR SUPER POWER?

Last week, my daughter and her kindergarten class took a fieldtrip to Kaleidoscope, a magical kid-friendly art studio, and I got to tag along as a helper. It's a place where imaginations can run free and creativity has no limits.

All the parent chaperones were positioned throughout the various rooms and instructed to help the young artists assemble their creations. They handed me a stapler and a roll of tape and stationed me near bins of construction paper, cardboard shapes, and ribbon.

After standing for several minutes with nothing to staple and nothing to tape, I passed some time by fashioning a cape out of a large piece of tissue paper and some ribbon. Then I made a cool hat – at least I thought it was cool – and struck my best Super Man pose with my fists on my hips. Apparently my marketing ploy worked. Soon I had a line of kids wanting their own capes.

My deal with them was that they picked out the ribbon, I would staple it on, and they could decorate the cape any way they wanted. And as I tied a cape onto each of the kids, I recited a little ritual that went something like this:

"This is your super hero cape. When you put this on you will have fantastic super powers. What is your special super power?"

"I can shoot fire out of my fingers," the first boy announced with a dramatic flourish of his hand.

I laughed. With two daughters of my own, my world is full of princesses and rainbows, which has fogged my memories of the warrior-like nature of boys.

"Remember, being a super hero is a big responsibility," I said. "What good can you do with that power?"

And with classic little boy enthusiasm and a karate chop to the air he said, "I kill bad guys!"

"OK, so, yes, protecting us from evil is a big help, now what other positive things can you do with your super fire power?"

He stared at me blankly, like I had just sucked all the fun out of the game.

"You know, what could you do to help people?"

Bewildered silence.

"Maybe you could cook food for people," I offered, trying to make it sound really cool. "Or maybe start fires for people who are cold."

"Yeah, that's it," he said with renewed interest. "I'll start fires for people. They can call me Fire Man!"

"Excellent, Fire Man, now go save the planet." And off he swooshed to make more art.

The next several kids in line were boys, each with comic book-inspired super powers.

"I'm the Ice Man," said one kid. "I freeze things."

"I'm super strong and can crush bad guys," said another.

And then a little girl stepped up and declared her distinctly sugar-and-spice-fueled super power, "I help flowers grow. I'm Flower Girl!"

The next girl in line said sweetly, "I'm Bee Woman. I help pollinate flowers."

For the next half-hour I was a stapler-wielding, cape-fabricating machine as the parade of super heroes continued – the boys leaving their super worlds strewn with super destruction, and the girls using their powers to spruce it back up.

In the final minutes of our session, the last little girl stepped up to receive her cape, and she would proceed to rock my gender stereotypes.

"And what is your super power?" I asked, expecting something fluffy and sugar-coated.

"Hot lava," she said confidently. "I shoot hot lava."

"And what good do you do with your super power?"

"I kill bad guys," she said, followed by a look that said "Duh!"

"Hmmm…let me see," I said. "You must have older brothers."

"Uh…yeah. How'd you know?"

"Just a lucky guess."

What a joy to meet all of those super kids who were super charged to go out and make the world a better place. They reminded me that we each have a distinct super power, and it's up to us to discover it and figure out how to use it wisely.

So, what's your super power?

"HOMELESS" ONE NIGHT— GRATEFUL FOREVER

I once spent the night before Thanksgiving in a homeless shelter in Milwaukee.

I had gone "under cover" for my university's magazine to get a glimpse of what it was like on the inside. What I encountered blew my narrow college-boy mind.

The church-based mission had moved into an old school near campus, and there was some concern about the "element" the shelter would attract. The student body and the homeless community were uneasy with each other. So I went to check it out.

I let what few whiskers I had at the time grow out for several days. I put on an old stocking cap and a tattered windbreaker and lined up with the rest of the men outside the brick building in the bitter Wisconsin wind.

Once the doors were opened, the new guys, like me, were plucked out of line and interviewed by a staff member who asked my name and age and if I had accepted Jesus Christ as my personal savior.

A long line of about 40 of us — black, white, young, old, able-bodied and frail — were escorted upstairs to a large open area that had been converted into a dormitory lined with rows of neatly made cots.

We approached a counter where we were given a basket, a towel and a set of clean blue pajamas. We were instructed to remove our street clothes, put them in the basket for safekeeping and then head to the showers.

It was a surreal scene as we filed out one-by-one from the other end of the bathroom. Some of the more tired-looking and hunched-over men seemed to walk a little easier and stand a little taller. And some of the roughest-looking characters didn't look so tough shuffling around in identical blue pajamas. It's amazing how a hot shower and a change of clothes can level the playing field.

I slipped under the clean sheets of my creaky cot and lay quietly listening to some of the men compare notes about which soup kitchens in town would serve the best Thanksgiving dinners.

Some laughed as they plotted their routes for the next day so they could hit more than one meal. Then it struck me that for most of these men, this was their family. They were a band of brothers who lived on the streets together and looked out for one another.

As I stared up at the ceiling that night, I felt overwhelming gratitude for my own family and a renewed appreciation for the luxuries of hot running water, clean sheets, and a comfortable bed.

Since that experience nearly 30 years ago, Thanksgiving has never been about food for me. It's about gratitude, not gravy, and what's in our hearts, not our bellies.

SWEET SMELLS OF SCHOOL

The anticipation of another school year came wafting into our home last week, packed into two shopping bags brimming with supplies — fresh boxes of No. 2 pencils, perfect pink erasers, unblemished folders, glimmering glue sticks and a short stack of tissue boxes.

Our soon-to-be-fifth-grader opened a slick, black, spiral notebook. She was drawn to it because "it looks like something a reporter would use." She ran her hands over the clean, smooth pages.

"I like the way it feels," she said. "It's like anything can happen, and then when you start writing, the pages kind of fill themselves. There's so much potential."

Then she closed her eyes and breathed in the freshness of the pristine notebook.

There's something powerful baked into the smell of brand-new school

supplies — something full of infinite promise.

Even the aromas of the classrooms and hallways of the school itself can create or trigger a cascade of memories the other senses can't match.

I have visited hundreds of schools throughout the country during my career, and, with a few exceptions, they all pretty much smell the same.

Every time I step into a school cafeteria the acrid smells of sour milk, baked mystery meat, and bleachy cleansers swirl into an unpleasant olfactory gumbo that assaults my brain's limbic system somewhere near the hippocampus. That's the spot where smells trigger memories.

Instantly I'm hurled back to third grade. I'm sitting at the lunch table nibbling on a crumbly peanut butter sandwich and an apple, while my friend Steve inhales potato chips, a Ho Ho and a can of lemon-lime soda wrapped in foil. His mother must really love him to send him off with such an awesome lunch.

In the corner, George the janitor stands ready with his mop, a bucket and a box of sawdust – just in case one of those nervous stomachs decides to heave back its lunch.

Over in the dank and musty gym, the woody smell of the floor mixed with odoriferous canvas high-tops and sweat-soaked cotton reminds me of that one glorious afternoon in middle school when we actually won a basketball game — the only one in four years of losses.

In the kindergarten room, the salty aroma of Play-Doh and the dusty scent of construction paper take me back to a time when I was five. My classmates and I sat with our eyes riveted to a tiny black-and-white television screen as we watched Apollo 14 splash safely back to Earth.

And the hallways always remind me of when my classmates and I would shuffle in after recess, shrouded in a cloud of Indian summer humidity with a distinct whiff of asphalt. I call it "Eau de Playground."

But there's nothing that would instill in me a greater sense of anticipation and creative potential than the sweet bouquet of an unmarked Big Chief tablet and a freshly sharpened pencil.

The smell of school is in the air. Imagine the possibilities!

MIDDLE CLASS DRAMA

It's just been one of those weeks. Stressed. Overwhelmed. And feeling that the wheels on this dilapidated bus are going to fly off at any moment.

When your world is being held together with duct tape, paper clips, and super glue, there's an ominous sense that we're just one tick away from collapse. And I use "duct tape" a little bit figuratively, but mostly literally.

How long will the duct tape on the van's bumper hold up? Will my backdrop that's held up with paper clips come crashing down during a performance? How much more super glue can I use on the chipped coffee mugs, plates, and bowls before they're considered toxic?

Occasionally being overwhelmed is part of a parent's job description. But some days are more anxious than others. When I look too closely or think too hard, this is what I see:

Maybe, if we're lucky, we can squeeze a couple more winters out of our

15-year-old roof. The van needs new tires before the snow flies. Have you priced tires lately?

I really should have an eye exam and have that suspicious flakey patch on the bridge of my nose removed by the dermatologist, but we've got pathetic health insurance. The crumbling front sidewalk is a sprained ankle waiting to happen. And my unexplainable habit of not tightening lids on jars will ultimately drive my wife crazy.

These are the things that keep me awake at night.

But just about the point where I feel like I'm careening toward the edge, I hear the rational voice of my good friend Kate who reminds me these are all just first world problems – examples of what she calls "middle class drama." Kate spent years conducting anthropological studies among the poorest of the poor in the Amazon and in Africa. She explains it like this:

If we were truly poor, we wouldn't have a home to maintain or a van to patch up with duct tape. If we were poor, we wouldn't have lame health insurance to complain about. If we were poor, we'd have a whole different set of anxieties like finding food for the day.

And, if we were really rich, we'd just throw some money at these problems and they'd be resolved. And we'd create some other high-class dramas to consume our lives.

Kate's right. In the big scheme of things, all of these worries are not all that bad. At the end of the day, we've still got a roof over our heads (precarious as it may be). My kids have shoes. We've got food in our bellies. We'll sleep on clean sheets tonight. And, as far as I know, my wife still loves me despite the loose lids on jars.

Here's another bit of wisdom that keeps me going through these anxious times. It's the lyrics in one of my favorite songs by The Who.

> "Pick up my guitar and play
> Just like yesterday.
> Then I'll get on my knees and pray
> That we don't get fooled again."

Let's not get fooled. All is well.

SURVIVALIST SHOPPING FOR THE FORMERLY COOL

All I wanted was a new pair of pants. Something casual and suitable for work. It should have been a simple, nearly pain free shopping experience – in and out.

"Pain free" is always the key for me when it comes to shopping, because there are few things I dislike more than shopping for clothes. It's right up there with shopping for shoes and watching golf.

My first and biggest mistake was veering from my reliable shopping habits. I foolishly ventured into new territory by visiting a hip and trendy store which I am neither hip nor trendy enough to enter. I just thought it was time to freshen my look – another monumental blunder.

I had no idea the sensory assault that awaited me as I opened the door and walked in. The blazing lights and overly ambitious signage with saturated colors and overwhelming heaps of inventory would have been oppressive enough, but it was the ear-splitting and teeth-rattling music that sucker-punched me.

When did clothing stores become dance clubs?

"ARE YOU FINDING EVERYTHING OK?" one of the perky young employees shouted at me over the rhythms of a pounding hip-hop tune that I could feel in my spleen.

I just shrugged in utter bewilderment that bordered on panic. But I was determined to complete my mission, so I made a dash for the men's section with a frantic sense of survival, like I'd suddenly been dropped into the Hunger Games of shopping.

As the chest-thumping soundtrack pumped overhead, I flipped through some racks of pants and shirts without really even knowing what I was doing, because I couldn't think straight.

Maybe that's exactly how the retailers designed the whole experience. They probably contracted a team of psychologists who recommended frazzling the shopper's nerves to the point where they just surrender all sensibilities and buy a bunch of stuff.

My heart was racing, and I was getting a little twitchy, so I grabbed a few items and headed for what I thought would be the comfort and safety of the dressing room.

No such luck. Dressing room lights and their surround-vision mirrors don't lie. There I stood face to face with a guy I swore was much younger when we walked in. A guy who once had really great hair and a healthy glow. But on that particular day I looked like a fidgety mouse with sallow, sun-damaged skin, and a glaring bald spot.

Who was I to think I could get away with wearing their tight-fitting plaid shirts and jeans that were already faded and ripped? I felt like I had entered a foreign country and couldn't speak the language. I was just a middle-aged fish out of water.

Suddenly I longed for the familiarity of some traditional hum-drum retailer that pipes in soothing jazz renditions of Beatles songs and employs soft spoken middle-aged salespeople who understand me.

I returned the clothes to the dressing room attendant and walked purposefully and quickly toward the door.

"THANK YOU," shouted a young worker dude. "COME BACK AND SEE US!"

Fat chance, I thought, as I broke free into the predictability of the suburban parking lot.

ROAD TRIP!

There's something about packing up the van and hitting the road with my family that sets my soul right.

We drove to New York and back over spring break — 2,600 miles round trip through farmland and cities and mountains and valleys. Along the way I dodged a thousand potholes and was entertained by scads of creative billboards. This year's two most popular topics were guns and Jesus.

Something profound hits me every time we venture out. It usually happens when my wife and kids are asleep, or buried in books, and I'm left with my thoughts and the hypnotic hum of the road. This time it was along an easy, open stretch of interstate in Indiana when I was reminded that life really is a road trip.

My wife and I try to teach our daughters to be flexible in all situations while honoring themselves. This can be difficult since we're still working on that ourselves. Traveling is a great way to practice.

You can plan all you want and map every inch of your journey and download all the right apps, but something always comes up. There are delays and detours and cracked windshields and flat tires and carsick children. Just think how boring the journey might be without a little shoulder maintenance and uneven pavement.

Sometimes you end up in a place you didn't expect, and sometimes it's better than you could have imagined. And, if you're open to it, you will always meet incredibly interesting people.

Sometimes, I don't really want to know where I'm going. I don't want to have a plan. It tempers expectations and leaves the canvas open for something totally unexpected and exciting.

On the highway of life, there will always be someone who drives faster and those who drive slower and, yes, those who haven't quite figured out that the left lane is for passing, and those who just don't care about rules.

There are those who make bad choices and seem to get away with it and those who get pulled over and pay a fine for it. Sometime you might be that person with the flashing lights in the rearview mirror.

There will always be someone with a newer, fancier car zooming by in the fast lane and someone with an old clunker limping along in the slow lane and others on the side of the road with their belongings on their backs who wished they had a car.

And just when you think you've had enough of the stresses of the road (or that your bladder is about to burst) there will be a reassuring sign in the distance with the promise of "gas — food — lodging" at the next exit.

Even if you're not up for learning how to become adaptable and flexible, it will be foisted upon you. The circumstances demand it.

Like the time we had to pull off the road during a tornado warning and seek shelter in a hotel that had lost electricity and had nearly all of its windows shattered by softball-sized hail. Or the time our transmission blew out in a small town on the first day of a 26-day tour, and two women named

Faith and Angel appeared (not making this up) and helped us get a ride to a nearby town where we were able to trade in our busted vehicle on a used van that we still drive.

Great family memories can be created under many circumstances, but often the real adventure comes from the twists and the turns and the jams. Life is what happens on the road between here and there.

PART III
THE GROOVY LADIES IN OUR HOUSE

ANGELS SHOP AT TARGET

Our five-year-old daughter Lyda told me an amazing story about how, when she was an angel in heaven, she picked Jeni and me to be her parents.

Lyda went shopping one day at the heavenly Target. It was August 13th. She remembers the date because it "felt like August, and it smelled like August. And, well, it really tasted like August."

She found Jeni on the "girl" shelf and me on the "boy" shelf, where we sat like statuesque busts, just "heads and shirts." She picked me first, she said, because she loves me "as big as the world."

"You had on a blue shirt and mom had on a purple shirt." Naturally. Our favorite colors.

"Then I picked out your bones, and your arms, and legs, and hair, and paint to color your eyes, and some peach-colored stretchy stuff for your skin. I even picked out your toes," she said proudly.

"How come you didn't get me some more hair?" I interrupted.

"Well, sorry," she said, "we were kind of in a hurry, and we were really hungry. It was about 5:30, and we had to get back to God's house to get something to eat."

"What did God serve for dinner?"

"Noodles, of course. We had noodles pretty much every night."

"Did you ever get sick of eating noodles every night?"

"No! God had lots of parmesan cheese and parsley. And we had milk, but that's about it."

"You said 'we.' Who else was with you?" I asked.

"There were other angels who helped me pick you out. Your dad helped me pick you out, too," she said. "He was the only boy helping me. But, there were about 12 girl angels who helped me pick out mom."

"My dad helped you pick me out?" I asked. "That must have been a long time ago."

"Oh yeah, it was before you and mom were babies. Because you've got to start as babies, you know. We took all the parts over to God's house and he put you together. I helped him a little, maybe this much," she said, holding her thumb and index fingers about an inch apart. "And then God put you in your mommy's tummy and he put mom in her mommy's tummy. And then I helped God get you and mom together, but that took a long time."

Yes, it took years for us to meet, but it's so cool and comforting to know that someone as wise and loving as Lyda picked us to be her parents.

And there's no need to worry about anything because she and God took care of the details long ago.

CELEBRATING MIRACLES

This week our family celebrated "Miracle Day."

It was five years ago that our then eight-week-old daughter survived a nearly fatal blow to the head by a screaming line-drive foul ball at a minor league baseball game in Wichita.

It's a humid summer's night. Our two-and-a-half-year-old sees stadium lights and gets excited. "Daddy, is that a baseball game? Can we go?"

Our family settles into some bleachers on the third base side. I'm not feeling too comfortable with our proximity to the action, so I opt to move the family farther back to a "safer" location. We settle in again.

A few minutes later I hear the voice of my long-dead father (a baseball nut and a stickler for safety) whispering in my ear, "Jim, it's a right-handed batter. Stay alert." I shrug off the heavenly warning.

Next pitch cracks against a wooden bat. Line drive heading right for us. Deer in headlights. I dive to protect our 2-year-old, Lyda. Jeni raises her arm to protect the nursing infant. Ball caroms off Jeni's forearm, leaving a nasty welt. It ricochets and clips the back of Willa's head, fracturing her skull in two places.

Screaming. Crying. A frantic scramble. Everyone OK? Footsteps approaching. Ushers. Officers. Willa is noticeably lethargic. Bump growing on the back of her head. They shepherd us out of the stands and into the ground level concourse. An ambulance appears. Paramedics. And, eventually, firefighters. EMTs examine and say she'll be fine. A firefighter makes eye contact with me, slowly shakes his head, and whispers, "I'm a dad, too. She's not OK. Take her in now."

As if all of that weren't surreal enough, a videographer from a local news station captures footage of the post-impact commotion. A week later the eerie images appear on the evening news in Kansas City – a bird's-eye view of Jeni stepping into the ambulance with Willa.

An hour or so passes as we move from ambulance to emergency room to a meeting with a hospital chaplain to trauma center, and we hear words that all parents fear. "It's serious," the attending doctor declares in front of the entire waiting room. I steer him out into the more private hallway where he continues. "I've seen this many times. If she lives…" (Wait…did he just say "if"?) "…she's likely to have permanent brain damage."

Our knees have gone wobbly and our stomachs are about to release their contents. Then he adds… "She'll probably need emergency brain surgery tonight. But we'll know more when the neurosurgeon arrives. He's on his way. It should be about an hour."

The longest hour of my life. And, strangely, one of the most amazing.

After phone calls to family, Jeni and I hold each other in the hallway. Lyda, who has been an absolute angel, pushes herself between us, puts one arm around Jeni's leg and one arm around my leg. She starts swaying and singing, "Let's stick together. Let's stick together."

Even though she's not quite three, Lyda is wise like a little Buddha and knows what our family needs. I tell her, "Yes, we do need to stick together.

And when your sister is better and we're home, you and I are going to write a song about this." (And we do.)

The neurosurgeon shows up, checks Willa out and tells us, "Yes, it's serious. Fortunately, she's got a squishy head. Her brain will swell and her head will expand with it. We'll put her in an induced coma for about four days to let the swelling subside. If all goes well, there will be no brain damage, and you'll be able to tell her about this at her wedding."

Other than six long days in the hospital, all went as well as could be expected. Prayers and good wishes poured in from family, friends, fans, and strangers from Australia, Africa, Europe, and all over the US. And we met about a dozen angels who helped us at every step. Today, Willa is a spirited, healthy girl.

There's no question that a miracle took place that week. I don't know if it was in Willa's healing or in the transformation that took place in our hearts. Because, after all, it is in our hearts where the real miracles happen.

To honor this miracle and to acknowledge that miraculous things happen every minute of every day, we decided to spread some of that love and hope by doing something for others every year on Willa's "Miracle Day." So, yesterday, the girls baked dozens of cookies, and we served them to the grateful guests at the St. James Place Community Kitchen.

After nearly two hours of helping clear trays and wash dishes, Willa said, "I never knew hard work could be so much fun."

Today is someone else's Miracle Day, and so is tomorrow, and the next day, and so on. Let's celebrate!

DADDY, WILL YOU MARRY ME?

When I arrived home from work the other day, our nearly-five-year-old daughter ran out the front door screaming, "Daddy's home!" She greeted me in the driveway with a proud grin and handed me a little white box.

"It's for you," she said, as she was about to burst with excitement.

I knelt down and opened the lid to find a dazzling bejeweled ring nestled inside. All I could say was, "Wow!"

"Daddy, will you marry me?" She blurted. Then she reached up, hugged me around the neck and kissed me.

I squeezed her tightly and told her that was the coolest thing anyone had said to me all week.

"Are you sure you want to marry a musician?" She just squeezed me tighter.

I wanted to stay frozen in that moment forever. The same way I wanted to freeze the moment when I asked her mother to marry me. It is now packed away securely in my Daddy Hall of Memories. Forever.

After I assured her I was beyond flattered and thrilled she had chosen me, I reminded her I was already married. Oh well, on to the next adventure, and she skipped off to blow bubbles.

As a father of daughters, I can't help but think about how my girls will bob and weave their way through relationships on their journey to find a life-long partner or not. And I wonder what kind of partner each one will choose.

My wife and I are continually amazed how two kids from the same parents can have such wildly different personalities. Our older daughter exhibits many of the classic "first born" qualities like rule-follower and people-pleaser, while our younger daughter tends to make up her own rules. They are going to handle relationships differently, and they'll attract different kinds of suitors. So, I approach each one a bit differently.

I think it's safe to say that kids learn best about relationships from their families. And that's made me acutely aware of how I interact with my girls – how I talk with them, how I touch them, how I praise them and discipline them, how I laugh with them, and how much leeway I give them to make their own mistakes. It's made me attentive to how I interact with my wife. I want them to know how people should treat each other and, in our case, how parents interact to make a loving partnership work, even when times are challenging and tense.

None of us is responsible for another person's actions. That includes our children. They are independent human beings with their own free will. As much as we'd like to think we have some control over what they do and say, we don't. Of course, as parents our responsibility is to love unconditionally, even when our kids frustrate us. And our job is to teach our children well and lead by example. But who they become depends on them.

I wrote a song for my daughter Lyda after she was born. It sums up my feelings about parenthood. The sentiment applies to both my girls and to any parent who is trying to figure out the balance between holding on tightly and letting go. It's called Daddy's Girl. Check it out sometime.

LESS IS MORE

Today marks the end of a three-year-long experiment. What started as a family exercise in frugality and creative belt-tightening turned into a motivating challenge and, ultimately, a real sense of freedom.

As 2009 drew to a close and winter set in, we braced ourselves for the typically slow period in the cycle of our family-run business. We knew it was coming and things would get lean. But that year we were feeling the recession and our budget got so tight that we had to sell one of our cars. It wasn't an easy choice, but one we knew we could handle since we had been spending most of the hours of most days together as a family.

"We'll see if we can make it six months," we decided.

Not only did we get an influx of cash from the sale, we instantly started saving on fuel, insurance, and maintenance.

Having one car may seem like plenty – or even a luxury – to those who don't own one. But for two adults living in the mass-transit-challenged suburbs, it was challenging.

At the six-month mark things were going well, and we were getting the hang of our new lifestyle, so we decided to shoot for another six months. At the end of a full year with one car it was now the new norm for us and rarely an issue. Occasionally I had to rent a car for week-long tours when the girls couldn't join me.

Then about this time last year, we agreed that it was time to get a new car. We scoured the web and the car lots and zeroed in on something we liked. When it came down to purchase time, Jeni said she was uneasy, and the thought of taking on another car payment made her sick to her stomach. Long ago I learned to trust her intuition, so we scrapped the idea and proceeded to squeeze out an additional year of savings.

Now that I've got a conventional job that requires me to be in the same place at the same time every day, and I'm getting wimpy about the prospect of riding my bike to the bus stop on frosty mornings, it's time.

Today we take possession of a second car. It's not "new" by any stretch (a 2001 with more than 125K miles), but solid enough to get me to and from work.

So, here's some of what we learned in the past three years:

It feels really great to purge possessions.

It feels even better saving money while purging.

We can get by with a lot less stuff than we thought we could.

Having less stuff can be liberating.

Things don't create happiness.

And perhaps the greatest lesson – pointed out by my wise and lovely bride – was this: Having one vehicle caused us to strengthen our creative problem solving skills. It pushed us, as a family, to negotiate and work through challenges. It helped us improve our communication and be more aware of each other's schedules and needs.

Once again, Jeni's intuition was spot on. And it seems her intuition to ask me out on our first date was right, too. Tomorrow we celebrate ten years of marriage.

LESSONS FROM JON THE BOX

There are few things as promising as a simple cardboard box.

It can be a fort, space ship, treasure chest, boat, cabin, castle, or cave. It can be a limousine used to drive your stuffed animals to dinner with the queen. You can hide in it. Sleep in it. Eat in it. And, I suppose – if you wanted to – you could store some stuff in it.

Kids immediately recognize the enormous potential of an empty box, and they see it for what it really is – the best toy ever! And sometimes it's a whole lot more.

We moved into a new house two months ago, and for the weeks leading up to that monumental event and in the months since, boxes have infested our lives.

When our six-year-old daughter saw how much fun my wife and I were having "playing" with all of those boxes, she wanted one of her own. She

adopted a sizable, sturdy carton and promptly named it. In marker, along one of its sides, she wrote, "Hi. I am Jon the box. Please don't take me. I love you."

She packed all of her stuffed animals into the comforting protection of Jon's cardboard walls. Then she unpacked them. She drew on Jon – and talked to him. Then she packed herself inside for a while and closed the flaps.

"Sometimes he does tricks," she tells me with a serious face, like transforming into a grand banquet table for a royal tea party.

Jon made the trip over from the old house and currently gets shuffled from room to room in the new house. I frequently catch myself referring to our adopted box as "him," which pretty much means he's become part of the family.

Moving from one home to another is one of those life events that is stressful, exciting, and emotionally charged all at once. While we were thrilled for a change and a new environment, we were sad to be leaving so many memories behind. It was hard on our girls, too. They didn't have to change schools, but we moved out of the only house and neighborhood that they've ever known.

It's a good thing Jon was there to help us cope with the change in a way that only a box can. Although I've tripped over him and cursed him a few times in the dark, there are a few bits of wisdom that I've learned from Jon the box.

- It's nice to have a reliable place to preserve our memories – whether it's in a physical location or simply in our minds.
- Occasionally a fresh, clean canvas allows us to cut loose and create.
- There's comfort in a quiet hideout – a retreat where we can shut out the din of the madding crowd and let our thoughts run free.
- We all need a sturdy, dependable friend who listens more than talks.
- And sometimes it's really cool to be square.

FEEDING YOUR NEIGHBOR

Our seven year old asked if she can build a restaurant in our front yard and serve meals to the homeless. She wants to call it "Eating House for the Poor." She's even drawn up a design and an action plan.

I love her gentle and generous spirit. The idea sounds great to me, but there's a little issue with the city. It's not easy explaining zoning laws to a child.

But what has been surprisingly easy is talking with the kids about poverty and what it means to be poor. They seem to get the concept – not so much the "why" of poverty, but the reality of it. For them, the solutions are simple.

"You always tell us to share, so let's share some of what we have with them," our daughter says.

Sounds simple to me. And logical. And Buddha-like. And Muhammad-like. And Christ-like. And…well…human-like.

According to history and most world religious texts, the poor have always been with us and always will be with us. As long as there are imperfect human social structures, there will always be those "with" and those "without." I just happen to think it's our obligation and honor to understand and care for the poor, not make them scapegoats for larger issues.

According to some modern-day pundits and part-time Facebook philosophers, the poor have simply chosen to be poor. Their poverty is merely the consequence of their own bad choices.

"They're lazy," they say. "Can't they just pull themselves up by their bootstraps?"

I've heard these lame arguments far too many times. Indeed there are people who manipulate every social structure. For every person gaming the system to get food stamps to feed her children, there is a person benefiting from corporate welfare, hiding millions offshore, and paying no taxes.

I have worked with marginalized people much of my adult life – on the Navajo nation in western New Mexico, in Central American villages, and in a job placement program on Kansas City's east side. I have met very few lazy poor people. Most are bustin' a hump. Many work more than one crappy job and still come up short. Then they are forced to swallow their pride and line up at the food pantry to bridge ever-widening gaps.

Sure, there are lazy people who refuse to work. I've met some who have comfortable corporate jobs, too. But from my experience they are the exception and not the norm. Most people have an innate desire to work and have purpose, and then there are those who have been beaten so far into despair they don't know how or what to do. It's easy to talk about someone else's motivation when you've got three square meals, a hot shower, and a roof. The reality is that the system is broken. The opportunities available to me are not available to all.

Once again, I defer to the wisdom of children. Their natural instinct is to offer a hand up without asking a bunch of questions. Because that's what neighbors do for each other. And as Sesame Street and Mr. Rogers so appropriately taught us – we're all neighbors!

I believe in nurturing my children to be responsible citizens who contribute to a healthy, civilized social structure, to do what's right for the common good. I prefer to teach my kids to love and then stand out of the way and follow their lead.

TALKING 'BOUT MY GENERATION

Sometimes I think our girls actually enjoy it when my wife and I reminisce about our childhoods. Other times they just tune us out.

Like when I go off on a tangent about classic rock, I'm sure this is what they hear: "Blah, blah, blah, the Rolling Stones, blah, blah, blah, Bruce Springsteen, blah, blah, blah, The Who."

As a father, it's my duty to pass along cultural iconic lessons, and I hope they will sink in and my girls will care about them, too.

My father did the same thing for me. I remember him reminiscing about Glenn Miller and Count Basie and how he once took a date to see Louis Armstrong at Kansas City's Pla-Mor Ballroom in 1937. He was so put off by the 75 cent ticket price he considered passing, but finally decided it was worth paying that much to see a legend.

I got a glimpse of my father's youth and his personality (and his frugality) through his music. And because he shared it with such passion, I learned not only to appreciate, but eventually to enjoy his music.

He once took me to Starlight Theatre to see the Mills Brothers, a revered vocal quartet who were then past their prime. I remember my father's excitement when the aging singers shuffled out on stage. Seeing the show didn't mean a lot to me, but I was excited for him. And when I heard them perform, I understood.

What Louis Armstrong and the Mills Brothers were to my father, The Who is to me. The band members were and still are among my musical heroes, so I was beyond ecstatic when, on the day before my 15th birthday in 1980, I went to see The Who at Kemper Arena with some of my buddies. The Pretenders opened for them in what would become one of the best concerts I've ever seen.

The buff and handsome Roger Daltrey belted out the anthemic lyrics as he whipped and twirled his microphone. The gangly Pete Townshend bounced around like an acrobat performing his insane windmills on guitar. And the statue-like John Entwistle, who rarely moved his feet the entire show, tore up the frets on his bass.

Having inherited my father's Depression-era frugality, I had grumbled about the $12.50 ticket price. It was the most I had paid to see a show (until the Rolling Stones came to Kemper the next year, and I coughed up a seemingly staggering $17 to see them!). Both shows were money well spent. I'd call that a bargain.

Fast-forward to 2015, and it turns out that The Who and I both hit 50 the same year. They celebrated the golden anniversary of the release of their first hit single, and I observed a half century of life. But after Daltrey suffered a serious illness, The Who had to postpone their tour, and we didn't get to celebrate our milestones together until last month. It was so worth the wait.

My wife and I couldn't think of a better way to celebrate than to bring our daughters to see these rock legends. My girls were mildly interested since they were familiar with some of the songs, but when they saw those over-70 rockers tearing it up on stage, they were riveted.

At one point my older daughter reached back to grab my hands and had me wrap my arms around her as we swayed to "Baba O'Reilly," a song she recognized and knew that I loved. Our 8-year-old, who complained about how loud it was (even through earplugs), climbed up into my arms during the finale, "Won't Get Fooled Again," which was a song that she and I have danced to dozens of time in the living room. We screamed and pumped our fists.

This was a priceless moment — sharing my passion for this band and this music with my girls, who genuinely enjoyed it. And sitting around us were other fathers with their kids creating their own inter-generational musical memories.

The day after the show, my older daughter asked if she could download some of The Who's music. I couldn't help but feel a minor proud daddy moment knowing that the rock 'n' roll seeds I had planted were actually taking root.

And I imagine that someday, if Taylor Swift is still performing in her 70s, our girls will take their children and tell them about the time their parents took them to see her for the first time. And the torch of our family's passionate musical history will have been passed.

A LITTLE PUPPY LOVE

We had about a dozen really good reasons not to get a dog. Most of them turned out to be valid – but, in the end, not one of them mattered.

Dogs are expensive. They require food, treats, crates, squeaky toys, harnesses, leashes, heart worm pills, and trips to the vet.

Dogs, especially puppies, require lots of attention. Let him in. Let him out. Did he pee? Did he poop? And when they're exploring their new world, they're incapable of discerning the difference between soccer cleats and a chew toy.

And we weren't sure if our family was ready — if the girls were responsible enough to pitch in with the extra feeding and cleaning and walking.

But the biggest drawback was me. I can be a bit of a curmudgeon and have been known to cling to the illusion that I'm in control. There's something distinctly out-of-control about having an unpredictable pack animal in your home, not to mention one that tracks in all kinds of allergens and minuscule crawly things.

So, with all of those seeds of doubt stewing in our indecisive brains, my wife decided we could ease into dog ownership by fostering some rescued puppies. Sort of a no-obligation doggie test drive. I reluctantly agreed.

Our first fosters were brothers, 7-week-old Rottweiler/bulldog mixes. Highly spirited and cute beyond description. And to help with the transition, the rescue organization provided us with a crate, exercise pen, bedding, and food.

I'm not going to claim it was all giggles and grins. It wasn't. A whole new level of chaos erupted in our house, as the front room turned into a kennel. The pen was set up in front of the dining table, and the room became littered with toys and training pads and food bowls. It was loud and smelly.

Since it was my wife's idea, she volunteered to get up in the middle of the night to let them out. The girls heaped lots of love and guidance on the pups, and kept them fed and watered. I helped by shuffling around the house muttering to myself as I picked up various shredded items and wiping up puddles of pee.

After three weeks of climbing over baby gates in every doorway and having all our conversations revolve around canine welfare, I was thrilled when the pups were adopted by loving and eager families.

I seemed to be the only one who savored the regained order and heavenly silence. Our girls were sad and said the house seemed empty. Lucky for them, the rescue called with news of a litter of 10 abandoned pups. My wife's big heart couldn't say no, so she and the girls persuaded me to take in two males.

They were 5-week-old mutts — possibly a mix of Rhodesian ridgeback, beagle, American Staffordshire terrier and wire-haired dachshund — the color of toasted waffles with lots of saggy skin to grow into. They wrestled and snarled and snapped at each other for hours on end before snuggling together for long naps.

The bigger of the two was adopted after three weeks. His brother was so distraught that he whimpered and whined for days as he moped around heartbroken. The girls named him Dobby after the doe-eyed, sock-loving, floppy-eared house-elf in the Harry Potter series.

As the weeks passed with no interest in adopting Dobby and as we all grew to love him, it became apparent he was meant to be with us. By the time we made his adoption official, he already seemed like a member of the family.

Dobby is pure love. The more you dish on him, the more he gives it back. He greets us every morning with licks and kisses. His whole backside wags when we come home from an errand. Whenever I hug my wife or one of our girls, he wiggles in between us so he can share in the love.

He was five cuddly pounds when we first met. Now, at 6 months, he's about 45 pounds and growing. He rings a bell that hangs from our back door when he needs to go out. He wants so desperately to please, and he doesn't hold grudges.

As the only two males in the house, he and I have bonded. We do testosteroney things like wrestle on the floor, chase each other in the yard, and play tug-of-war.

Our older daughter says that the house just seems more active and lively now that Dobby is part of the family. We walk more. We play more, not just with him, but with each other. And because he's so social, we've met lots of new dogs and people.

We had exchanged no more than some waves and hellos with our neighbor across the street. But since Dobby arrived, we've become good friends with him and Foxy, his Jack Russell terrier. He watches Dobby when we're away, and Foxy hangs out in our backyard.

If you try hard enough, you can come up with hundreds of reasons not to do anything in life — adopt a pet, get married, start a family, accept a job offer, whatever. But you only need one good reason to take a leap of faith.

PART IV
THE ONES WHO RAISED ME

BACON IN THE OUTFIELD

The smell of fried bacon reminds me of baseball. And for that peculiar olfactory connection, I can thank my father.

The spring I turned 11, he introduced me to his own brand of rawhide therapy – a process to get my leather ball glove ready for action after a long, dry winter. The first step involved a pound of bacon and a frying pan.

My mother favored a heavy, cast iron skillet to fry everything. When the bacon got crispy, she'd pluck it from the crackling fat with tongs and lay it gingerly onto a bed of paper towels. Then she'd lug the pan over to the sink where she kept an empty orange juice can. Very carefully she would pour the hot grease into that can and place it on the window sill to cool.

After a couple of hours the bacon grease would coagulate into a smooth white and speckled balm. My father showed me how to dip my fingers down into the can and scoop up some of that slimy goodness and rub it right into my baseball mitt. He taught me how to massage it deeply into the grain of the leather and work it from the palm up into the fingers and how to bend and twist that glove back and forth. I performed this little ritual every day for about a week until my mitt was soft and flexible.

When you're playing defense in baseball and you're crouched down waiting to field a ground ball or running to catch a pop-fly, the last thing you want is a rigid glove. Otherwise the ball might smack the pocket, bounce right out, and leave you with a fat lip. What you want is a glove that is an extension of your very hand, one that is pliable and snaps shut when it's supposed to – like a Venus Fly Trap.

My mitt was as limber as they get, and I played organized baseball with it for a few years with a team that never posted a winning season. We were a hapless band of dreamers aptly sponsored by a local Optimist club. Each guy on the team was good enough to be in the league, but never good enough to make any of the contending teams.

That particular year I had been relinquished to the outfield early in the season following an unfortunate infield incident that wasn't entirely my fault.

I was playing second base with adequate aptitude – I could field most grounders and throw accurately about half the time. So, I felt pretty confident when the batter hit an infield fly ball that was otherwise routine, but really high. I called it and planted my feet, but as I watched the ball climb, I immediately lost it in the glaring midday sun.

I had seen this happen to other kids and thought, "Come on! It can't be that bad."

Until your retinas have been seared and rendered useless by ruthless ultraviolet rays, you just don't understand. I closed my eyes, put my glove over my head and hoped for the best. The ball landed with a thud in the dirt about a foot from my right shoe.

My coach was so frustrated that he called time out and waved me over to the dugout. As I trotted over to him, one of my team mates ran past me with an apologetic shrug and took my place at second base. My coach was

pulling me from the game and didn't even have the decency to wait until the end of the inning. (This was the same coach who pitched miniature marshmallows to us during pregame batting practice, so that by game time the baseball would look HUGE and, he presumed, easier to hit. Interesting theory, but it didn't help.)

So, there I stood in the outfield for the remainder of that long, hot season, eagerly waiting for some action that might redeem me. Some days the only thing I caught out there was an occasional whiff of bacon grease wafting up in the humidity. That's when I'd very nonchalantly bring the webbing of the mitt up over my face and pretend I was concentrating on the game, but secretly, I'd be slowly inhaling that oddly comforting aroma. Soon I'd be drifting back to the breakfast table and daydreaming about a couple of glistening basted eggs.

There was someone else in our house who loved my baseball mitt nearly as much as I did – our dog, Babcock. Whenever I would leave my glove lying around after practice, I'd be sure to find it clutched between his front paws as he sat licking the leather over and over and over. He never chewed on it; he just sniffed and licked every inch of it with a twinkle of ecstasy in his eyes.

That baseball glove served me well for many seasons until I foolishly left it out in one too many rainstorms that eventually ruined its lining.

Although I eat more veggies than meat these days, the smell of bacon still brings back fond and fabulous memories of my younger, freer, more nimble spring days on the baseball diamond. And forever I will fondly associate spring, bacon, and baseball.

I Have Become My Father

I love the Royals and baseball.

So did my dad. He was a hometown boy fascinated by the craft and mechanics of the game. He loved its cerebral nature with all of the statistical nuances.

"It's a thinking man's game," he would remind me.

He also loved the sights and sounds and smells of the ballpark, but he had little use for the peripheral pageantry he considered a distraction from the beauty of the sport. He was unimpressed by mascots and scoreboard graphics and between-inning gimmicks. He was a purist who logged every pitch on a scorecard he would buy on his way through the turnstile.

However, one tradition he relished was the seventh-inning stretch because it involved singing. And he loved to sing, especially "Take Me Out to the Ballgame." But as soon as it was over, he was back to business. "Watch the ball at all times. Keep your head in the game," he would say.

My dad seemed more impressed by clever players than by exceptional athletes, and delighted in victories that involved superior tactics over brute force.

Being a tactician himself, my dad carefully plotted out our trips to the ballpark. We'd leave the house with plenty of time to ensure an early arrival and to fit in a stop at the grocery store to pick up a bag of peanuts to share at the game. He was frugal like that.

As soon as we would roll into a parking space, he would start planning an exit strategy. He had a serious aversion to post-game traffic, because he couldn't sit still very well. For someone with a passion for a slow sport like baseball, he was not a patient man.

If the Royals piled on a comfortable lead or fell helplessly behind, we would head for the exits by the end of the seventh inning or the middle of the eighth. In the event of a close game, he'd take us to the concourse level to watch the last inning so he could whisk us away ahead of the crowd. I'm not sure I ever saw the final out of any game when I was a kid.

For better or worse, I have inherited my father's impatient streak and his tactical obsession involving large, crowded events. Like him, I feel a certain rush of satisfaction at the mere thought of out-maneuvering the masses by getting a five-minute jump and finding the quickest way home using shortcuts and backstreets.

But, like him, in my desire to avoid being inconvenienced by a slow-moving moment, I just might miss something cool, like the Royals' ability to stage a late-inning miracle. Or more important, I might miss sharing a memorable moment with my girls.

If there's one phrase I fear my daughters will remember me by, it's "C'mon! Let's go! If we leave now we can beat the crowd."

But the truth is, there is little redemption or glory in beating the crowd. It just cheats my family and me out of enjoying the gift of the present.

So, I've asked my girls to point out when I start jingling the car keys and looking around for the nearest exit. I've given them permission to remind me to just chill out and enjoy the show.

STANDING FOR GOOD

The more stories I recall about my father, the cooler he gets. Maybe that's because as I gain more experience as a parent, I'm growing to appreciate all that he did for us.

He was a man of faith, integrity, and action. And I know where he stood on the issues of his time.

In 1955, he and 15 other white lawyers formed a committee to lobby for the inclusion of African-American and female attorneys into the Kansas City Bar Association. They crafted and signed a letter to all members urging them to vote for a change that was right and just.

Because his name was attached to that letter, my father received many notes of support and several nasty ones containing ugly epithets. Some of those hateful letters came from lawyers he knew well.

Years later my father admitted to shredding those nasty letters because

he knew those men would later regret that they'd ever sent them. He didn't want there to be any evidence that might embarrass them. That was my dad. He wasn't vengeful or a grudge-holder.

Following the riots that rocked American cities in the spring of 1968, my mother and father became active in Kansas City Crisis, a group organized to create dialogue and seek peaceful solutions to the racial tensions. When the group met at our house, the little kids would gather and play games in an upstairs bedroom while the adults engaged in intense discussions in the living room or around the dining room table.

When fire damaged the home of some family friends, my parents insisted that they move into the house we had just bought in another neighborhood. We had not yet moved in, so it made perfect sense for our friends to stay in the vacant house until they could rebuild. The fact that our friends were black did not sit well with many of our new neighbors. By the time our family moved in several months later, there were neighbors who would not speak to us.

Perhaps the most indelible image I have of my father was after the outbreak of the first Gulf War. He was standing on a street corner on the Country Club Plaza, wearing his overcoat and woolen Irish cap, and holding a sign that read, "Honk for peace!" He was a proud World War II veteran who had served as an Army officer in an artillery unit in

North Africa and Italy. Because of his front-row seat to the brutality and inhumanity of war, he knew more than most the importance of pursuing peaceful resolutions.

My father didn't have to preach the lessons he taught me — he just lived them. I can only hope our daughters never have to ask my wife and me where we stand on the issues of our time. I trust they will instinctively know the importance of a life guided by compassion, tolerance, and inclusion, and that they will always pursue the common good.

LOVE RULES

My sister Trish has been married three times — to the same woman.

The first time was 18 years ago in New York in what she calls a "spiritual but not legal" celebration in the presence of family and friends.

The second time they made it legal before a judge in Oregon. But several months later, Oregon changed its mind and issued them a refund. "Without interest," my sister adds sarcastically.

The third time was two years ago in a joyous, legally binding ceremony in Seattle with more friends and family.

The marriage of these two determined women has been a simple matter of fact for our two daughters, who have always known their aunts as a loving, committed couple. Their marital status has never required an explanation.

What's there not to get about love? "Duh," as my girls would say.

Last month the Supreme Court officially acknowledged what we've always known. Aunt Trish and Aunt Pam's love is real. Their love is legitimate. Their love matters.

Their right to marital benefits is as legitimate as the rights my wife and I enjoy, and their relationship has had no effect on the definition of our marriage. If anything, it serves as a model of how to sustain love and fidelity under the strain of being treated like marginalized citizens.

As parents, my wife and I have tried to build our family upon the tenets of love, respect, and acceptance of all people. That's how I was raised.

My parents intimately understood divine love and used it to propel them to the front lines of desegregation and the civil rights movement. Despite opposition from some in their church-based circles, they knew they were doing the right thing.

They exemplified a loving God and embodied the Christ who said, "Love your neighbor."

Because of them our family knows that love never excludes — not for race, religion, income, gender, or whom you choose to marry. There is no "worthy" or "unworthy." It doesn't keep score. It doesn't favor a flag or an anthem or an ideology.

Love sows peace. It never drops bombs or flies airplanes into buildings or invades another country or burns down churches. Love has no need to cling to weapons as a symbol of power and freedom. Love is power. Love is freedom.

Love lifts up the downtrodden. It does not blame the poor for being poor. It does not measure the length of one's bootstraps or the effort with which one pulls on them. It does not deny access to health care, food, or shelter.

Love comes from a place of abundance where there is plenty for all. It has no use for excess or hoarding.

Love surrounds hatred with light and renders it powerless. Only fear thrives in the shadows. Only fear lashes out in an attempt to dishearten and control others. Only fear seeks revenge and has the audacity to call it justice.

The love our family knows is free. There is nothing you can do to earn it or lose it.

I respect the right of others to disagree with my beliefs. But I also know that the Supreme Court has done the right thing by ruling in favor of inclusion and nudging our nation in the direction of love.

Just as I watched my parents put their love into action, our daughters are listening and watching our words and actions as they frame the context of this historic moment.

I intend to leave no doubt in their minds about where I stand. I choose love.

PUSHING BOUNDARIES WITH ZAZ

Every kid should have an Aunt Mary.

Someone to confide in and someone who understands you when Mom and Dad just don't get it. Someone to hang out with on a Friday night, who doesn't mind if you stay up late, eat junk food, and crash on her couch. Every kid deserves to know a trusted adult who doesn't treat you like a kid.

That was my Aunt Mary Byrne. She died last week after 85 years of living life on her terms, with little care for what others thought.

She was the only one of six girls who didn't get married and have a brood of her own, and she relished her role as the quintessential fun-loving, single aunt to 31 nieces and nephews who adored her. Even though that was a lot of ways to divide her love and attention, each one of us felt special when she was around.

My dad dubbed her Aunt Zaz (I assume because she was full of pizzazz), and she lived up to the hype.

She talked loudly. She dressed loudly. And she lived loudly. She wore wigs, bright red lipstick, and so much Tabu perfume that when she hugged you, the scent lingered in your hair and nostrils well into the next day.

She was glamorous, like someone on TV. She was a former homecoming queen who became a successful professional living on her own in an apartment. She was our very own Mary Tyler Moore and Auntie Mame rolled into one.

Her apartment was the coolest place to hang out because she had a pool, plus a fridge full of TV dinners and soda, and a can of whipped cream that you could spray right into your mouth. She instigated poker games that lasted for hours and would pretend to look the other way when we snitched a few sips of her Miller High Life.

Every year at Christmas for more than two decades, she gave each one of us something she knew no one else would — a crisp $2 bill, which became one of her trademarks.

For nearly 40 years Aunt Mary worked as a trusted lobbyist for the city of Kansas City to the Missouri General Assembly. People all over the state knew and respected her. But none of us kids knew what a lobbyist was. All we knew was that when the chambers were in session, she would load up her Buick with cans of Topsy's popcorn and slabs of ribs and head to Jeff City. She often regaled us with stories of backroom deals brokered at late-night parties.

Being a scrapper and a negotiator in her professional life also helped her as she successfully battled both colon and breast cancer. She credited her recovery to her positive outlook and lots of prayer.

Now that I have daughters of my own, I realize how important it is for them — and for us — to have at least one Aunt Mary. Someone to allow our kids to test boundaries and challenge the rules, while allowing us to maintain some facade of parental authority.

Our girls need to know that there are other adults, related and not, who will listen and laugh and love them when they need a break from us. Fortunately we're surrounded with fabulous role models who would make Aunt Mary proud.

SHE
NEVER
STOPS
DOING

Last week my mom fell and broke her hip. When you're 86, you don't have many options.

"I don't want the surgery," she said. "It scares me. Just give me the pain medicine."

Her doctor agreed, saying she likely wasn't strong enough to make it through surgery. He recommended hospice care. Somehow that wasn't a surprise.

My brother and I sat with her in the emergency room as we waited for them to arrange transportation to the hospice house. Through her medicated fog, which was interrupted by an occasional dagger of pain, we were able to have a coherent conversation that pretty much sums up parenting.

She started by apologizing and saying how guilty she felt about my siblings and me having to care for her. This coming from a woman who spent the better part of a decade being pregnant, suffered two miscarriages, birthed and raised eight babies, and put a hot breakfast on the table six days a week. Oh yeah, and a hot supper.

"Guilty? After all you did for us? It's only right that we should take care of you," I said. "I can't even comprehend how many diapers you must have changed. And they weren't disposables."

She waved me off with her frail, bony hand. "That was nothin'. Besides, that was all I had to do. It's not like I had another job." My mother has been known to exaggerate, but she excels at understatements.

When people would ask how she and my dad managed so many children, she was fond of saying, "Oh, we didn't know any better. That's just what you did." As if that explained everything.

"We had planned on having a dozen kids," she said. "But after Sheila was born, the doctor told me not to have another, that my body couldn't handle it. But I told him, 'You're wrong. I've got to have one more.'"

Against her doctor's recommendation, she had one more. And that baby was me. I'm grateful she also excels at being stubborn and defiant.

"I feel like I should be doing something," she said as agitation and restlessness set in. "What's the point of me just laying here?" But then she paused, no doubt catching herself in what she perceived to be a lapse of faith, and added, "But who am I to say? It's in God's hands."

"Doing" is all she knows. She's been doing for others her entire life, and her doing is part of the reason she ended up in the emergency room. She was up folding laundry without her walker when she fell, even though someone else cleans and folds her clothes. I can't say I blame her, though. It's one of the few things that gives her purpose.

And I think purpose is a huge part of what being a mother is all about. They never stop loving and doing. They never stop worrying and feeling guilty. They never stop being mothers. And we never stop being children.

A JOYFUL LIFE WELL LIVED

My mother died last month, less than a week after falling and breaking her hip. Her health had been failing for years, and the fall was just too much for her to overcome.

For better or for worse, her mind was sharp the night they took her to the emergency room, which means she was alert and aware of her dwindling prospects. And when she brushed off the idea of surgery and chose the open bed at the hospice house, she had to have known the full weight of that choice.

My seven siblings and their families drove and flew in from all over the country, many of them making it in time to say goodbye or at least to hold her warm hand one last time.

A bunch of us packed in around her bed the night before she slipped away. As I looked around the room, I was struck by the beauty and sheer volume of our family tree, the branches of which had all sprung from this once strong woman whose body now lay withered and fading.

Some tears sneaked up on me as I watched my nieces gently massage their grandmother's feet and affectionately stroke her snow white hair as they whispered their goodbyes. Those simple acts of pure love made everything right.

Aside from those few tears that night, I have yet to have a good cry over my mother's death. I haven't had the big "bawl" that I had after my father died more than 20 years ago.

At first I was feeling a little guilty over my lack of tears, but those thoughts were quickly replaced by a calming sense of gratitude — for the 86 years of my mother's life and for the life she gave us.

It sounds strange to admit it, but I have felt real peace and joy since her death. And it comes from knowing she is finally pain-free, and that her deep faith and spirituality comforted her in her transition.

Last year my mother told one of my nieces how jealous she was of her friends who had already passed on.

"I don't understand why God keeps kicking me and punching me," she said. "I just want him to put me on his back and carry me home."

She's home now. And she left this good life surrounded by people who love her.

In the end, what more could anyone ask for?

Acknowledgments

I gratefully acknowledge the *Kansas City Star*, where all but two of these essays were first published. A version of "Memories Rooted in George Brett's Lawn" first appeared in the *Albuquerque Journal* under the title "Brett's Clippings Made a Fan." A version of "Dance of Healing – Dance of Peace" first appeared in *Radical Grace* (a publication of the Center for Action and Contemplation).

My spirit glows with gratitude for my lovely bride Jeni and our daughters Lyda and Willa who fill me with their inspiration, love, and support. And I wouldn't be the human I am without the nutty clan that helped mold me – my seven siblings and my swarm of nieces, nephews, aunts, uncles, and cousins. They've stocked me up with years of material.

I'm eternally grateful for the love and support of my in-laws, Gene and Peggy Schmidt, who raised the only human who was bold enough, smart enough, and caring enough to join me on this journey.

Many thanks to Sharon Hoffman, my editor at *The Kansas City Star*, for giving me a shot and challenging me to be a better writer, and to Phyllis Theroux for her guidance and encouragement, and to Susan Motley for her thorough and encouraging editing of this collection, and to Charlie Miley for his whimsical illustrations, and to Rob Peters for his amazing attention to detail and monumental patience through the design process.

And to all who provided words of wisdom and super helpful editorial and design feedback – Robin Blakely, Dawn Downey, Danielle Young, Dave Rebeck, Joanie Shoemaker, Jo-Lynne Worley, and Margo Posnanski – thank you!

My heart soars with admiration and appreciation for my brothers from other mothers – my wingmen, band mates, and musical collaborators Mark Thies and Dean Ottinger. We've covered many miles together and performed in sweaty festival tents and sweltering parking lots to the stages of word-class performing arts centers. They've taught me much about life and love and how to be a better human.

Special thanks to Ben Worth, whose wisdom training and guidance helped me rediscover my roots so that I could stay grounded long enough to allow this project to unfold at its own pace.

And thank you for taking time to read these words and becoming part of my story. Someday I hope to read yours.

DISCOGRAPHY

- Bop Bop Dinosaur (1998 – re-released by Warner Nashville in 2005)

- Stinky Feet (1999 – re-released by Warner Nashville in 2005)

- Ooey Gooey (2000 – re-released by Warner Nashville in 2005)

- Stinky Feet Live! (DVD – 2001)

- Pick Me! Pick Me! (2002 – re-released by Warner Nashville in 2005)

- Mr. Stinky Feet's Christmas (2003 – re-released by Warner Nashville in 2005)

- Mr. Stinky Feet's Road Trip (2005)

- Mr. Stinky Feet's Road Trip Live (DVD – 2007)

- Upside Down (2008)

- Swimming In Noodles (2010)

- Smiles Ahead – Cool music for cool families (2015) Producer

- Heart Beats – Feel good songs for families (2016) Producer

Check out Jim's music and performance schedule at
www.jimcosgrove.com
@mrstinkyfeet

MORE INTERESTING STUFF ABOUT THE AUTHOR

Award-winning kid rocker Jim "Mr. Stinky Feet" Cosgrove is a former journalist and corporate public relations professional who had the good sense to get a "real" job helping kids laugh and learn.

Throughout a mostly accidental 20-year career, he has performed more than 3,500 shows in 30 US states, Canada, Mexico, Germany, Italy, England, and Spain. He's performed at festivals, bank openings, schools, world-class performing arts centers, pizza joints, with symphonies, twice on the south lawn of The White House for the annual Easter Egg Roll, and once in front of the "intimate apparel" section of a department store.

He was born the youngest of eight children to two Irish-Catholic parents who admitted they "didn't know any better." He was raised in the Brookside neighborhood of Kansas City within walking distance of St. Peter's Elementary where Sister Jeanne taught him the beauty and symmetry of a well-diagrammed sentence. He spent most of his childhood summers swimming and playing baseball with a bunch of other Catholic kids at the Jewish Community Center.

Cosgrove earned a bachelor's degree in journalism from Marquette University and a master's degree in creative non-fiction writing from the University of New Mexico.

He's lived in Missouri, Kansas, Wisconsin, New Mexico, and Tennessee, and tends to fall in love with every place he visits. And he once took a three-week test drive as a Benedictine monk in a monastery near Santa Fe.

His colorful employment history has included frazzled substitute teacher, over eager waiter, super attentive bar tender, swinger of a sledge hammer for a contractor, meticulous house painter, greasy spoon cook, harried bus boy, conscientious deliverer of newspapers, slacker grocery sacker, detailed lawn manicurist, eyebrow-less antique lighter repairman, squeaky window washer, groovy summer camp counselor, record label mogul, spokesdude for a telephone company, lone male staff writer for a women's magazine, grammar-geek editor, inspirational public speaker, voice actor for various holiday-related tchotchkes, and celebrated bingo caller.

A few of his favorite journalistic assignments included flying with a medical mission group into a remote village at the bottom of Copper Canyon, Mexico; "covering" a nude juggling festival, which turned into another feature about nudist RV owners; riding all night on the reservation with a Navajo police officer; helping wranglers prepare a mule team for a pre-dawn trek into the Grand Canyon; making snow angels with revelers in Moscow's Red Square at three in the morning; and interviewing a husband and wife grave-digging team who met on the job.

His musical influences include Woody Guthrie, Pete Seger, Joni Mitchell, The Who, John McCutcheon, Jimmy Buffett, and scads of singing nuns throughout 17 years of Catholic education. Oh, and Springsteen.

CPSIA information can be obtained
at www.ICGtesting.com
Printed in the USA
LVOW11s1757210218
567418LV00002B/356/P